MORTGAGE FOR MAVERICKS

The Business Owner and Self-Employed Guide

To Funding Your Dream Home and Investment Properties

AMANDA MADSEN

Amanda Madsen -- 1st ed.

ISBN: 978-1-954757-08-0

CONTENTS

INTRODUCTION

I wrote this book with my fellow creators, risk-takers, and passionate entrepreneurs in mind. This is a unique group of people wanting to be in charge of their own destinies to live and create wealth. They don't want to sit behind a desk all day but instead share their knowledge and passion for improving others' lives. They are independent and creative-minded, including various professionals such as wedding planners, DJs, hairstylists, and lawn care specialists, to name a few. Entrepreneurs can decide when and how to do business, therefore enjoying a sense of freedom. I was one of those who didn't like to be told where to be, how to be, and when I could go home. It seemed restrictive and repetitive. I was fired from every job I ever had that required me to punch in and out. I was miserable doing something that didn't fulfill my passion.

So, first of all, I want to congratulate you. If you are reading this book, you are one of the bold, driven, and committed entrepreneurs that make up small businesses, which have a considerable presence in our economy across the country. You deserve the opportunity to purchase a home and have the ability to create wealth from owning homes.

Somewhere along the line, you've been told that getting a loan as a self-employed borrower is challenging. Perhaps you feel you don't make enough money or don't know how to structure your taxes to qualify for homeownership.

I'm here to give you all the information you need to make you feel comfortable with the concept of owning a home. Sure, there are loan officers that simply don't want to deal with self-employed borrowers because it is a little more work on their end. This book will guide you on finding the right professional to set you on the path to homeownership, one that will work with you to achieve your goals.

You may be wondering why I'm the person to help you. I have been where you might be right now. I started out as a self-employed hairdresser and a single mom, motivated by building my own wealth, choosing my own hours, and still being there for my daughter. As my business grew, I was making more money than I had ever anticipated. Yet, the thought of owning a home still seemed so out of reach. I was overwhelmed by trying to understand the process and saving the amount of money required to get my foot in the door. I would get anxious thinking about owing taxes. And so I surrendered to the fear that since I was self-employed, I just wouldn't own a home. Not until I left the beauty industry for the mortgage industry did I find out I could have bought a home several times over.

How does a hairdresser turn loan originator, you might ask? I always knew I didn't want to be doing hair when I was 65, so my eyes and ears were always open to other career options that would still allow me the same freedom and financial stability. One of my hair clients was a loan officer making tons of money at the peak of the real estate market. I was intrigued but hesitant about going from chatting, cutting, and styling to crunching numbers and getting people into homes. I dove in headfirst, knowing I was starting from the ground up. I knew I needed to build my business to reach my goal of buying a home. And I became passionate about advocating for other self-employed borrowers trying to do the same thing. Now that I see how truly easy my goal would have been to attain, I kick myself over and over. Like many other entrepreneurs, I simply had no idea where to get the information or turn for help. So I didn't even entertain the idea of homeownership. I just decided it wasn't for me.

Being in this industry has opened my eyes to the very real possibilities that exist. It gives me joy and happiness to help well-deserving business owners purchase homes and investment properties. In the following pages, I will highlight simple steps for setting up your taxes and building up your book of business to position yourself for loan approval. After purchasing an investment property and the home of my dreams, I'm prepared and passionate about taking you on a similar journey. It's time to embrace the opportunities that await you, armed with the knowledge and confidence to make homeownership a reality.

- Amanda Madsen
"The Maverick Mortgage Maven"

CHAPTER ONE

EXPLORING ENTITIES

It is essential to understand the different types of entrepreneurship, how we get paid, and how those intertwine with qualifying for a loan. The lender will look at each scenario differently, depending on how you are getting paid and how you set up your taxes. The first step is to determine which category you fall into and how that will play into the loan process.

Sole Proprietor

One of the most common types of entities that I encounter for self-employed borrowers is the sole proprietor. This is someone who has not set up an LLC (Limited Liability Corporation), an S Corp or is not a 1099 (Independent Contractor). This is a very basic entity. Nail technicians are a great example of sole proprietors. They typically rent a booth in someone else's salon and write off all of their equipment such as nail polish, files, brushes, and UV lights, all while enjoying the freedom of being self-employed. Other common sole proprietors include hairstylists, DJs, wedding planners, landscapers, graphic designers, and freelancers. These are people who choose to keep things simple when it comes to taxes without being bogged down by the ins and outs.

Sole Proprietor Pitfalls

A common challenge for sole proprietors is the desire to write *everything* off, so they don't have to pay a lot in taxes. There has to be a delicate balance. As a loan officer, I am looking at the adjusted gross income when qualifying someone for a loan. For example, let's say a nail technician made $100,000 in one year. They then write off $30,000 in booth rental, equipment, and cell phone expenses. As all of these items become deductions, the income amount required to qualify for the loan reduces.

Nobody wants to pay a lot in taxes. So there is a considerable inclination with sole proprietors to write off as much as possible. A client of mine who is a mechanic is the owner of a very successful business. It is growing, he is hiring employees, and his gross income was almost one million dollars. By the time I received all the deductions from his CPA and started the loan process, it left him with a qualifying income of only $2,000 per month! There is not much room left for buying a home with that amount of income, is there?

Don't get me wrong; I was once one of those people. I didn't want to pay taxes, and there were times I wrote so much off that on paper; I only made $11,000 a year. Obviously, I was living off more than that. To buy a home, you need to increase your income on paper by lessening the number of deductions. I help my clients develop a game plan with just the right balance between deductions and income to set them up for successful loan qualification.

If you are just entering the self-employed domain, keep in mind that most lenders will go off an average of two years of taxes. If you go in blindly and write everything off for two years straight, you will have to start from square one to gain qualifying income. That is why it is essential to dedicate time and understanding to your taxes early on for your loan officer to get an accurate picture of your income, and ultimately, into a home.

1099 - Independent Contractor

An independent contractor could be a real estate agent, or a contractor subbed out by a general contractor. These types of companies choose to pay their employees through a 1099 because they don't want to be accountable for paying any withholdings on their taxes. Like sole proprietors, independent contractors can write off anything they purchase to perform their job. Again, they need to be aware of that fine line when writing too much off. Home loans work the same way as car loans; you have to prove that you are not a risk and earn enough to make the payments. You simply can't write everything off and still expect access to all the fun things you want to do and have in life. Working with an experienced loan officer and CPA will ensure the balance you need to qualify for a home loan as an independent contractor. There is a trade-off; you get the freedom of working for yourself and controlling how much you make, but you have to pay Uncle Sam.

Brick-and-Mortar Business Owners

The brick-and-mortar business owner is a slightly more complex type of entrepreneur. They have taken on a lot more risk. They have higher rents and may even own buildings. Their business typically does well enough to pay for employees and liabilities and still makes enough money to be considered successful. Their taxes will be structured differently, usually in the form of an LLC or an S Corp. This type of business owner may have a lot more to write off. If so, they also must be aware they made a lot more money in doing that.

The Dream Team

If you haven't noticed by now, the common theme for ALL self-employed borrowers is focusing on the adjusted gross income and how that plays into qualifying for a loan. The more you understand what the lender is looking for, the closer that dream home is to reality. And oddly enough, that understanding can keep catapulting you to buy more, create more, and get more. It's really that easy with the right team in place. As a loan officer, I view myself, my borrower, and my CPA as the equation's three main components. We work together to determine your goals and arrive at a comfortable mortgage payment and the required income. The CPA uses this information to create a legal document, which is then turned over to me for loan qualification purposes. I am always happy to talk to borrowers and CPAs to create plans, even setting borrowers up for success in upcoming years. Even if you have already done your taxes as a specific entity and aren't quite there yet, I can help you get there. It is a perfect opportunity to start the dialogue about the next year, embrace what that is going to look like, and what you might have to compensate for in paying taxes. The result is worth it in terms of moving forward with security, wealth, and assets in your life.

For the average person, buying a home is the #1 most expensive purchase of their life. Most homeowners don't realize what a valuable asset that home becomes. As a self-employed person who is already taking this journey of controlling how much wealth you accumulate, owning a home is the next logical step because your return on investment is more significant than anything else. Markets are moving and growing astronomically at this time. People who I helped get into homes years ago are now sitting on hundreds of thousands of dollars in equity. This money can be used in times of crisis or simply to invest in another property. Statistics show that any person who purchases a home becomes more financially successful than someone who rents.

Whether you are paid 100% commission, a member of the gig economy, an entrepreneur, or an influencer, you fall under the same general requirements when it comes to qualifying for a home loan. Open lines of communication with your CPA and loan officer to determine appropriate write-offs will take you far in the pursuit of homeownership. Surrounding yourself with the right team members can help you navigate the delicate system of checks and balances to help you reach your goals.

Want my help? Book a complimentary "Dream Funding Plan" at the website listed below.

On this call, I will...

*** Learn your investment or funding goals.**
*** Suggest best practice options according to your goals.**
*** Help you avoid pitfalls and common mistakes that sabotage approvals.**
*** Give you a clear path of action so you can get funding with confidence.**
*** Provide you with my best recommendations and direct you to the best resources, even if I'm not the best option.**

CHAPTER TWO

CPA VS. LENDER PERSPECTIVES

Most of my understanding of taxes and income for the self-employed came as I immersed myself in the mortgage industry. I jumped from a creative world of doing hair into a financial, competitive, "no room for error" world. I felt like a fish out of water, and because my personality drives me to learn everything I can, I immediately dove deep, knowing the more informed I was, the better I could perform and serve my clients.

As an advocate for the self-employed home buyer, I need to discuss CPAs and lenders' different perspectives and the challenges presented from both sides. Armed with the knowledge to navigate through the crucial time of preparing your taxes, you can set yourself up for an approved application.

One of the top challenges self-employed borrowers face is writing everything off. Doing this can severely impact your future ability to purchase a home. I find that self-employed people are often less willing to set themselves up for success and get in their own way for many reasons. Perhaps they don't want to dedicate the time to understanding and organizing their finances in a way that shows they make enough income. Even their attitudes can hinder their ability to get a loan. Many self-employed borrowers discredit themselves when it comes to how much they make or may have the misconception that lenders simply "don't want to deal with the self-employed." That is why it is crucial to meet with a lender and have discussions to bust these myths. We can help you clear up the disconnect you might have between gross income and adjustable income less your expenses, giving you the confidence to see yourself as a homeowner.

FAQs

Q: How many years of taxes do I need?

A: This question has a couple of answers depending on the loan type. FHA, VA, and USDA loans will always require a two-year average of income from your taxes. If you go with a conventional loan, they will need two years of taxes, up to five years of being in business. After this, you can go off of one year, which benefits the borrower since business and profitability should increase each year. But keep in mind, if you come off a high year and then show a loss the next, this will be a red flag to the underwriter and bring the home buying process to a halt.

Q: Why do I qualify for so little? I can't even find a house in that price range!

A: This question is often asked with anger and disbelief. It all boils down to how much you wrote off in expenses. This is where we have to examine the lender's perspective. Overall, lenders view self-employed borrowers as having a higher risk than W-2 borrowers. They strive to go above and beyond to give you homeownership and need you to provide more proof and follow the rules a bit more to gain this valuable asset. We all know that we can adjust our taxes and how much money we make to avoid paying. But the caveat is, you don't get a house if you write everything off and show very little income. A home is one of the most significant purchases you will ever make. Sitting down with a knowledgeable lender can make the process less frustrating as you begin to understand what they are looking for.

The Lender Perspective

The first step in the home buying process is often one that a lender feels uncomfortable with. We're not CPAs, and we are not trying to give our clients CPA advice. Our job is to educate the client on how we have to look at income according to guidelines set forth by the government or the investor that will be giving them money for the home loan. The CPA looks at things very differently. I ask my clients to gather all of the information required by their CPA and bring me the numbers once the CPA is finished. I can tell them what they will qualify on and give pointers on how to increase income while still having the benefit of a write-off. I have conversations with the CPA to fill them in on our goals and strategies to help guide the client and leverage them to purchase a home. At the end of the day, the client has to decide what they are comfortable doing. I often ask, "Are you comfortable paying more taxes and then getting a home? Or are you more comfortable forgoing the payment of more taxes and then not getting a home?" The conversations continue between the client, myself, and the CPA to gain clarity moving forward.

I have a borrower that I have helped for some time I spoke of in a previous chapter. He is a very successful auto mechanic who makes almost a million dollars a month in gross income from the shop and cuts himself a paycheck. Once he got done with all of his taxes and expenses, the poor guy only showed $2,000 a month in qualifying income. It was a huge shocker to him when I had to say, "After all of the changes you have made over the past few years, you now actually make less than you did previously." That can be a hard pill to swallow. Even though I made suggestions on how to structure things differently three years prior, he was resistant to listen or make changes to increase his income. I attempted to speak to his CPA, who was not very friendly or helpful. The one thing he had going for him was a low debt to income ratio. He qualified for a $150,000 loan, but there were no homes available in that price range. We had many conversations about how the current setup was hurting him, but he was unwilling to make any adjustments with his CPA at that time. He actually got money back on his taxes, which was a bad sign because it meant he really didn't make that much money at all. Ultimately, we ended up going a different route and getting him a home on a non-qualified mortgage, which we will discuss later in the book.

This is a good illustration of people's misconceptions about how much they pay themselves and how much they actually get to use as income. I always try to guide and educate my self-employed borrowers in a way that sets them up for success the following year if the current one just isn't working out in their favor. I want them to learn how to balance out or leverage expenses better than they have in the past. When you purchase items for your business, it helps to understand if it will be a depreciation purchase. Keep your receipts to hand off to your CPA to determine if it will be best to write it off all at once or spread out over some time. There is a balance in this process where you are creating enough income and giving yourself enough of a break so that you are not going bankrupt or paying the IRS for 10 to 15 years down the road. This heightened level of understanding not only helps you to buy a house but also helps you get approved for credit cards, car loans, or other things you would like to enjoy as a self-employed borrower. Your overall life is improved by being able to get credit or make purchases on credit.

The CPA Perspective

Being a hairdresser, I used to come across all types of people with various careers. One of my favorite clients just happened to be a CPA. She was brilliant and did a lot of taxes for people in the higher tax brackets. I used to pick her brain a lot since I was self-employed. I got a lot out of our conversations as I was still doing hair and transitioning into the world of mortgage. She gave me a lot of insight into the challenges she faced with her clients as they dealt with loan officers that didn't understand income that could be used on their taxes. I realized a gap in understanding between the lender and CPA that often led to a great deal of frustration for everyone involved. It allowed me to get ahead of the curve and take a proactive step in my industry to help self-employed borrowers get into homes.

She helped me understand that when CPAs are structuring taxes, they don't just go in and start deducting everything without the client's instruction. The CPA will do exactly what the client tells them to do. If you say, "I don't want to pay very much in taxes," the CPA will help you find a way to make that happen. Another one of her frustrations was that many loan officers didn't realize that depreciation is something you can add back into your income. All of those funds can be put back into qualifying income, ultimately making or breaking a file. I learned there were many inconsistencies in the way CPAs and lenders are required to do things. Even when it comes to business mileage, lenders can only give the client half of the CPA's calculation. Without being aware of these little nuances on both sides, the process can be highly stressful, and fingers get pointed with the accusation of, "You have no idea how to do your job!" As a lender, I now have a unique ability to understand both sides and the value of communication between myself and the CPA to reach the best possible outcome for the client, with the least amount of conflict.

The Importance of an Open Mind...

You have to be willing to give a little in this process. I can relate to what it feels like to be self-employed and to try to navigate financials. I absolutely hated dealing with my CPA when I was a hairdresser. I always ended up feeling inadequate and uneducated. I was just plugging along, buying products, doing hair, getting paychecks, and living life. But I wasn't paying enough attention to running my business in a way that would benefit me. I have found that most self-employed people shine in their skillset. Let's take martial artists, for example. They master their skills and teach their skills better than anyone. But when it comes to transferring over to a business mindset, it may be a struggle. This ends up being the reason why many of these businesses fail. I had the same challenges. The thought of working on profit and losses and balance sheets overwhelmed me, so I avoided those things like the plague. Those weren't the parts of my business that I was drawn to or found enjoyable, so I pushed them aside. Today, there are so many options to empower you to learn this part of your business.

There are classes you can take and applications you can use to help streamline the process. This new knowledge will only propel you and your business to do better. And if all else fails, there is no shame in hiring a good bookkeeper to handle it all for you. It can only enhance your business to add someone with a knack for accounting to your team.

You also must be willing to have an open mind when it comes to paying taxes. As I made my way through the mortgage industry, taking classes and learning from business coaches, one of them said to me, "Paying a lot in taxes isn't a bad thing. It means that your business is growing. And isn't that the goal of owning a business?" I encourage my clients to look at paying more taxes in a positive light. We should celebrate making more money and the freedom it brings to our lives. Perspective is everything!

An open mind is essential for each member of your home buying team. Understanding the blended perspective between the lender and the CPA is critical to get your taxes set up advantageously. Meeting somewhere in the middle is an excellent place to end up and will give you the results you have been working towards on your mission to become a homeowner.

Want my help? Book a complimentary "Dream Funding Plan" at the website listed below.

On this call, I will...

*** Learn your investment or funding goals.**
*** Suggest best practice options according to your goals.**
*** Help you avoid pitfalls and common mistakes that sabotage approvals.**
*** Give you a clear path of action so you can get funding with confidence.**
*** Provide you with my best recommendations and direct you to the best resources, even if I'm not the best option.**

Book Your Complimentary "Dream Funding Plan" at: www.AmandasDreamFundingPlan.com

CHAPTER THREE

BOOKKEEPERS AND ACCOUNTANTS AND CPAS...OH MY!

When it comes to preparing taxes for their businesses, most people aren't aware of the slight differences in specialties between bookkeepers, accountants, and CPAs. It's overwhelming enough to run a business...do you really have time to figure out which one of these services is best for you? Sure, the "three percenters" of the world, like Bill Gates, would know how to distinguish between the three. But until I got into the mortgage industry, I lacked the clarity to understand how each service could benefit my business. Most entrepreneurs want to do what they love, make money, and figure out how to count it later.

The Role of the Bookkeeper

A bookkeeper offers insight into the day-to-day financials of your business. The bookkeeper's primary roles include handling reports, purchases and sales, reconciliation of documents and balances, payables and receivables, and payroll processes. A college degree is not necessarily needed to perform these services. Having a bookkeeper eliminates the everyday hassle of trying to understand what is going on in your business from a profit and loss standpoint. Oddly enough, it isn't as expensive as you might think to add one to your team, and a small fee is worth the peace of mind. Especially with small transaction businesses, like restaurants, for example, a bookkeeper is an excellent choice. They specialize in handling the tediousness of multiple funds coming in and out daily.

The one limitation a bookkeeper has is their knowledge of the tax code. Unlike a CPA, they don't have continuing education to stay up to date on new tax laws. I would not recommend a bookkeeper when it comes to doing your taxes. Instead, the bookkeeper's skill set lends itself well to keeping the daunting, daily accounting tasks streamlined so that you can focus on other aspects of your business that you excel in.

The Role of the Accountant

An accountant takes things one step further than a bookkeeper. If you plan to grow your business, accountants can offer big-picture perspectives and projections via business planning. They are qualified to give tax advice, tax planning strategies, financial forecasts, oversights, and recommendations. If you are spending too much on one area of your business, an accountant can advise you where that money would be better suited for financial growth.

Since an accountant typically has a Bachelor's degree, they can be slightly more expensive than a bookkeeper. But they can do your quarterlies, taxes and provide projections which are all valuable services. If you're in a business with fewer, high-paying clients, an accountant is the way to go. Some business owners also hire an accountant to double-check the bookkeeper's work and offer insights and projections from there.

The Role of the CPA

A CPA has gone to college to become a "certified public accountant," one step above an accountant. Their standards are much more stringent. Each year, continuing education is required to maintain their licensure and keep up to date with new tax laws and how those apply to the tax form. They are trained in specifics such as depreciation, which is a huge benefit if you are trying to qualify for a home purchase. Can specific items (car, computer, office furniture, etc.) be put in the depreciation file and added back into your qualifying income? Since these can be complex scenarios, a CPA becomes essential when preparing taxes. If you pay taxes quarterly, a CPA will provide you with the coupons to send out and give you expectations of what you will need to pay, so you aren't slammed with a huge tax payment at the end of the year. In the case of an audit and issues with the IRS, a CPA can help you fight the audit and walk you through what can be a nightmare situation. If you have high volumes of income or have a tendency to "play in the gray," the IRS has the potential to wreck your world. Having a CPA to go to bat for you in those situations is well worth the higher price tag.

Knowledge is Power...

As a business owner, you should ask yourself the following questions to determine which of the above services are for you, whether it be just one or a combination of the three.

- How busy am I?
- What types of transactions am I doing?
- Where am I excelling? Where am I struggling?
- What is my risk level?

Some people want to be completely hands-off and have a bookkeeper to handle the details, the accountant to give business advice, and the CPA to handle taxes. If you have complicated deductions and are looking for peace of mind, a CPA might be the best choice. On the other hand, if your business is very "black and white" and "by the book," you can potentially save a little cash by hiring an accountant. As entrepreneurs, most of us are well aware of our weaknesses. For me personally, it has always been bookkeeping. Don't be afraid to reach out and have conversations with each specialty to determine how they can pick up the slack for you. The more conversations you have, the more successful your business becomes, giving you the home buying power you desire.

Want my help? Book a complimentary "Dream Funding Plan" at the website listed below.

On this call, I will...

*** Learn your investment or funding goals.**
*** Suggest best practice options according to your goals.**
*** Help you avoid pitfalls and common mistakes that sabotage approvals.**
*** Give you a clear path of action so you can get funding with confidence.**
*** Provide you with my best recommendations and direct you to the best resources, even if I'm not the best option.**

CHAPTER FOUR

CREATING WEALTH

As a self-employed person, diversifying and finding other assets to create wealth is not only essential but, in my opinion, fun. Given the current economy, being diversified in any type of investment portfolio can only benefit you. Real estate investment is a perfect niche in creating wealth.

Over the past eight years of being in the mortgage industry, I have noticed that housing prices have only increased. Real estate offers a great return on investment, and often, even more so than the stock market. That isn't to say don't invest in stocks. Cryptocurrency is hot right now and seems to be the next big thing. But many wise people that I surround myself with advised me to begin investing in real estate to diversify my portfolio.

Eight years ago, I met Tyler, who is now someone I consider a friend. He was only 21 years old at the time, and his dad owned several investment properties. He set an excellent example of entrepreneurship for Tyler, who had the desire to follow in his father's footsteps. Tyler decided to buy a duplex as his primary residence while renting out the other half. When you purchase a duplex and rent out the other side, 75% of that lease payment counts towards your qualifying income. The guidelines state 75% with the assumption that you will most likely have periods of vacancy. The income that you receive from your renter as you live there also helps pay for your mortgage. If you do it right, you could almost live mortgage-free! Tyler purchased his duplex through an FHA loan with only 3.5% down since it was serving as his primary residence. It was a great entry point into his own home AND investment property.

Tyler lived there for a little while and, when he got married, decided to buy a single-family home. I helped him get a lease in place for the half of the duplex he was moving out of, now giving him two lease options and doubling his income. The qualifying income from his employment, as well as these two new lease payments, helped him get into his next home. From a mortgage professional's standpoint, the two leases essentially wipe out the liability of the mortgage on the duplex so that the mortgage won't hurt you when applying for the next home.

In the first year of owning any type of rental property, the lease agreement counts towards qualifying income. The following year, you will file taxes on a Schedule E for investment properties. The income moving forward is then generated off of the taxes for future home purchases. Let's say you have a duplex that you have lived in for two years while the other side was being rented out. If you have filed taxes on that property, wrote everything off, and it shows a loss, that could hurt you. The goal is to have enough profit or rental income to wipe out the mortgage. One side of the income will be generated from taxes, while the other will be from 75% of the lease payment.

You may be wondering what Tyler has achieved present day. After buying a primary, single-family residence with his wife, they bought one more, sold that one, and purchased a bigger house. Later, they refinanced that home to buy an Airbnb in Bear Lake, Utah. It is a constantly busy resort town, and in the wintertime, snowmobilers are looking for places to rent. In the first few months, Tyler made enough to pay the entire mortgage for the year plus profits on top of that. Recently, Tyler sold the Airbnb and took all of the proceeds (roughly $200,000 in two to three years), and put them into a 1031 exchange to help avoid capital gains taxes. I have helped him every step of the way. His most outstanding achievement is now a fourplex that he just bought in Wisconsin for $150,000 cash. All of it is being rented out, and that money is nothing but profit! Strategy, strategy, strategy. This is one of the many reasons I love what I do.

I always wanted to do what Tyler did. I intended to buy my primary residence in Montana first, but that plan was derailed when I met my boyfriend. Throughout my journey in the mortgage business, I have learned that short-term rentals create more profit and revenue. Think of short-term rentals as Airbnbs and Vrbos.

Even if I wasn't buying a primary anymore, I still really wanted to get into something. So I began looking for short-term rental properties in Montana. The particular location was a busy, picturesque resort town with an abundance of lakes. I planned on purchasing this home as a "vacation home." Under this definition, if you are legitimately planning to visit this home for vacation purposes, you are only required to put 10% down, and you receive a lower interest rate. On the other hand, if you were to classify it as an investment property, at least 20% down would be required, and the interest rate would also be higher. Seeing as I loved Montana and eventually wanted to live there permanently after my boyfriend retired, it was an easy decision for me to purchase the home as a vacation property. I was excited to go and visit while simultaneously creating additional income through short-term rental tenants. For all practical purposes, my vacation home was being paid for by someone else! I've done everything backward my entire life. In this case, purchasing a vacation property before a primary residence worked out exceptionally well for me.

Starting with one property and leveraging your way into more and more gives you a feeling of excitement and empowerment on your entrepreneurial journey. Whether you choose a half and half primary residence/rental duplex, vacation home, or long-term investment property, the qualifying income you earn can catapult you to the next level of investments and, ultimately, profits. Anytime I help someone get into a house, I remind them that I can always assist them in acquiring another one, building their portfolio, and creating an abundance of wealth.

Want my help? Book a complimentary "Dream Funding Plan" at the website listed below.

On this call, I will...

*** Learn your investment or funding goals.**
*** Suggest best practice options according to your goals.**
*** Help you avoid pitfalls and common mistakes that sabotage approvals.**
*** Give you a clear path of action so you can get funding with confidence.**
*** Provide you with my best recommendations and direct you to the best resources, even if I'm not the best option.**

Book Your Complimentary "Dream Funding Plan" at: www.AmandasDreamFundingPlan.com

CHAPTER FIVE

CREDIT SECRETS REVEALED

Now that we've covered what your taxes need to look like, we are going to shift into the actual, clear-cut requirements for getting pre-qualified and going through the mortgage process.

Income

Income will be reviewed by your loan officer and the underwriter based on a two-year average for a self-employed borrower. Even if your first year is low and your second year is high, we will take a two-year average up until you reach a five-year history of being in business. After that, we can go off one year for Fannie Mae or Freddie Mac loans or the same two-year average for an FHA program. As previously mentioned, this will not be based on gross income and will include all deductions.

Credit

Credit is currently at a 620 minimum score, and the name of the game is trying to get the highest score that you can. This will, in turn, help you get a better rate, which equals a lower mortgage payment. Borrowers often misunderstand how to build and maintain credit and how it can be easily manipulated. So if you understand the basics of how credit will be scored, it helps you move your credit in a higher direction if you are getting ready to purchase a home.

The first component is credit history. This includes what you've had on your credit and for how long. The longer you have had any line of credit open, the better. Opening up a new credit card will ding your credit and look like a new tradeline for two to three years. You don't ever want to close one of your longest-running credit cards because it significantly helps you in building credit.

We also look at credit depth. Perhaps a borrower only has three tradelines. Their credit depth is minimal in comparison to someone who has 14 different tradelines over their credit history. You should aim to open up new creditors less frequently and maintain long term credit history with a select few to build an excellent credit score.

Lastly, the frequency of credit use comes into play. How often are you using your credit? Are you a person that maxes out your credit every single time? Do you have a hard time paying it off? No matter what limit you are given, there is a delicate balance in using your credit. If you go above 50% of your limit, it will start hurting your credit. The goal is to try to maintain about 30% or pay it off to zero. I believe that credit cards for daily expenses are the best route. I encourage people to use them daily and then pay them off when the balance is due, especially if you earn points or mileage in the process. Debit cards are more vulnerable to hacks or identity theft. Credit cards also offer the security of disputed items being removed from your account. So use your credit card freely and talk to your creditor about when they report your payment to the credit bureaus. There is usually a two to three-day gap. For example, if your credit card is due on the fifth, by the seventh, or eighth, the credit card companies have sent out your history for that timeframe. And that is when your bank's new settlement statement comes out. If you were to pay it off on the exact due date and turn around and use it within those two to three days, you have created a new balance. So there's this little, unknown gap I like to talk about. You can basically have your credit history report at zero while using your card often and frequently. It's all about learning how to play the game in terms of usage and how it is going to be reported to ensure a score that is always high.

I typically tell my borrowers to pay off a credit card balance NEAR the end of the month (anywhere from the 22nd to the 26th) to see a significant jump in credit score since credit is reported on the first of the month. Another tip is to ask a trusted family member or friend to add you as an authorized user to their credit card. This can be extremely helpful. Perhaps you are trying to build your credit, but your credit score is only 650, and you don't have the most extraordinary credit history. When you are added as an authorized user on someone else's card, you immediately get all of their credit history. So if they have had the card for 14 years and are in good standing, your credit report will reflect that as well. Make sure that the person you choose has a really low or no balance. Otherwise, that debt to income ratio can be held against you when purchasing a home. With this little authorized user trick, your credit score can boost as quickly as one month!

Types of Credit That Help Build Your Score:

1. **Installments** - These include auto loans or signature loans that are paid down to an ending balance.
2. **Credit Cards** - Also referred to as "revolving credit."
3. **Mortgages** - These weigh heavily on your credit score. If you are late on your mortgage, it dings your score and will be very difficult to get removed.

This trifecta is essential for improving and maintaining your credit score. When it comes time to make a purchase, the higher your credit score, the lower the interest rate. Keep in mind that annual payments you make, such as car and homeowner's insurance, are also reflected in your score. That is why it is so important to nurture your credit to improve future transactions throughout your life.

Credit Myths

People tend to cringe when someone says, "We've got to pull your credit." There is a common misconception that this will negatively impact your credit score. When you're in the space of searching or qualifying for mortgages, those inquiries are not going to have a significant negative impact. When you search for a home, there is more leniency so that borrowers can feel safe to shop around for a good rate. In the world of mortgage, pulling credit is not adverse in terms of hitting or deepening credit. An excess of inquiries for other purchases can hurt you, though. For example, let's say you are shopping for a new car, and the dealer pulls your credit through 20 different financing agencies for one purchase. That will undoubtedly ding your credit, and it will take some time to have those removed. On the other hand, a mortgage originator pulls and then re-pulls your credit to determine where you are and how you are building credit strategically within the same entity.

Credit repair companies do exist, but many of them are fraudulent or just not very good. Be mindful of minimizing how many inquiries are pulled no matter what you are buying. Choose a loan officer to work with and stick with them. The mortgage companies do an excellent job of keeping our fees competitive, so you don't have to shop around.

Another misconception is that you can frivolously use your credit in the same way you always do while getting approved for a mortgage. Once you start the credit process in a mortgage, your loan officer will be alerted of any new attempts to open credit. If you try to buy new furniture or a car during this timeframe, there is a high likelihood it could kill the house deal completely. I have even had clients who forgot to pay a credit card bill during the loan process and could no longer purchase the house. You will still be responsible for the fees, the inspection, the appraisal, and anything else that has already taken place. But you won't get the house. Don't just wait until the ink dries; wait until the loan is fully funded and recorded before you attempt to go out and buy anything on credit.

Lastly, many new borrowers think that opening up many credit cards will build credit. I had one client in particular who was acquiring more and more credit cards to try to increase his credit score. He came to me and said, "I've been working on my credit, and I have my down payment. I'm ready to go." Upon pulling his credit, it revealed a low score. The credit cards with the most weight on your score are the major companies like Visa, Capital One, US Bank, and American Express. Opening up an Old Navy card, for example, could actually hurt your score. Most people don't realize that a brand new credit card dings your credit for the first year or two. Only after year three does it really start to have any sort of positive impact. My client also had a Capital One card account that he had never used. It was just sitting open, and he wasn't even sure where the card was or if he had ever gotten one. Not using accounts can also affect your score negatively, especially with the major card companies. My client wasn't aware of any of this. He said to me, "I've learned more about building my credit in this 20-minute conversation than I ever have in my life." He was very thankful, and I let him know that we could have his situation turned around in a month or two, bringing him closer to the 700 price bracket and getting him a more favorable rate.

One little-known fact is that the older the derogatory credit is, the less it weighs on your score. Someone may have an account sitting in collections for three to four years and think that paying it off is a smart way to build credit. It is actually more impactful to focus on the new things you are acquiring. The same goes for bankruptcy. As bankruptcy reaches the maturity of 7 to 10 years on your credit, it weighs less and less. I encourage my clients to focus less on what they can demolish and more on what they can build anew since not having enough positive credit will also bring your score down.

Business Debt

Many entrepreneurs choose to put business debt on a personal credit card. If you have a snow removal company, it might be tempting to put that brand new truck on your personal account. But as a business expense, that is now counting as a liability in your debt to income ratio. I encourage business owners to put business debt on a business tax ID that will not show up on personal credit or a credit report. A CPA or accountant can help you to make the transition. If you pay all of your business debt consistently through a business account and show that through 12 months of bank statements, we can reduce or remove that in your liability. This will open up your buy ability and give you more leverage when purchasing a home. By keeping this in mind and the other credit tips and secrets we have discussed, you will be able to acquire more and build your business better.

Want my help? Book a complimentary "Dream Funding Plan" at the website listed below.

On this call, I will...

*** Learn your investment or funding goals.**
*** Suggest best practice options according to your goals.**
*** Help you avoid pitfalls and common mistakes that sabotage approvals.**
*** Give you a clear path of action so you can get funding with confidence.**
*** Provide you with my best recommendations and direct you to the best resources, even if I'm not the best option.**

Book Your Complimentary "Dream Funding Plan" at: www.AmandasDreamFundingPlan.com

CHAPTER SIX

THE LITTLE-KNOWN BENEFITS OF BANK STATEMENT LOANS

As of this publication, we are coming out of the 2020 COVID pandemic. There have been many changes in our country, including a significant amount of job loss. Mortgage companies are faced with trying to figure out if it is safe to lend to people with investment properties. We've given renters the ability to stay in someone's home even if they can't pay their rent. This causes a huge problem for the property owner, as they are forced to make payments without receiving any rent money, and they probably never will receive back pay.

Until now, we have talked about qualified mortgages, or "QMs," as they are referred to in the mortgage industry. These are loans that follow Freddie and Fannie guidelines, FHA guidelines, VA guidelines, and USDA guidelines. They each have their own minor nuances but follow the same general regulations across the board. But now that we are coming out on the other side of the pandemic, some things have shifted and changed when it comes to mortgages for self-employed borrowers.

Non-qualified mortgages (non-QMs) are great alternatives right now for a few reasons. They follow similar guidelines but definitely break the rules regarding what they will allow and not allow. For example, let's say you wrote everything off on your taxes and want to buy a primary residence. You don't want to make that adjustment on your taxes and have to pay more. Well, there are mortgages available called bank statement loans. You can provide your last 12 to 24 months of bank statements, and your mortgage professional will go off the deposits you have made versus what is on your taxes. This will change how much you qualify for in a way that benefits you. I have personally done these mortgages for people that are wanting to buy their primary residence. Earlier in the book, we spoke of my mechanic client who had plenty of money but only $2,000 of qualifying income when it came down to it. We ended up using the bank statement program to help him get his home. Pre COVID, the interest rates were much higher for this type of loan. But it was still a benefit for him to acquire the house, gain some equity, and secure an asset that he can use to leverage and pivot in the future.

One of the other obstacles recently is that Fannie Mae and Freddie Mac have strongly limited the ability of people to own investment properties. And literally, in the midst of doing some of my loans for people in a refinance process, they shut it down and left it open for another investor to come in, but the rates were so ridiculously high. Buying down the rate exceeds the limitations that we have to follow in terms of fees. Those fees are put in place by qualified mortgage guidelines so that we're not adding a lot of costs onto somebody else's primary residence and causing the borrower to be in a more adverse scenario than needed. Now, Fannie Mae and Freddie Mac took away the option to go through them and get excellent rates but leave it wide open for other investors who are gouging the rates and the pricing just to get on the rate sheet. This ends up costing my borrowers over $15,000 to get a 5.1% interest rate. That is an obscene amount of a discount point. But it exceeds the limitations. Therefore, we have no option to give our investment property borrowers any ability to purchase or refinance homes.

Non-qualified mortgages end up working for many people, though they come with their own set of challenges. Your credit score plays a significant role in determining rates. The higher your score and the lower loan to value, meaning how much money you are putting down or how much equity is in the home, will dictate the rate. For example, if you have a 600 credit score, you will have a much higher interest rate, starting at about 7.25%. That is because your really low score indicates that you might not be the greatest at paying or managing your bills. On the other hand, a credit score of 760 could get you a great rate on a non-owner-occupied investment property. My best advice is to keep your credit score at 740 or higher, using the tips I have provided in previous chapters. It will be very individualized based on credit score and how much loan to value or equity you are starting the process with.

Non-qualified mortgages are still considering good buyers and their lend ability to avoid the subprime mortgages and the housing crisis of 2008. It is simply another option for people who don't want to show all of their income on taxes or write off their expenses. They offer some excellent choices, including adjustable-rate mortgages (ARMS), 30-year fixed, and interest-only loans, giving you the freedom to choose the loan that best meets your specific needs. Mortgage insurance is not required on these types of loans either. Even if you come in with 10% down, you still don't need mortgage insurance, which is another benefit. These non-qualified mortgage companies are seeing the struggles people are having, particularly after COVID. The guidelines for self-employed borrowers have become much more stringent. Fannie Mae and Freddie Mac ask for more documentation, such as profit/loss and balance sheets. All of this must match up with the income you are getting qualified on. Though I understand the reasons for this, I also find it unfair in many ways. That is why I am doing everything I can to help my self-employed borrowers acquire home or investment properties through alternative avenues.

I always say, "In this industry, it is better to get into a home however you can and position yourself later to make changes or adjustments." Most of my clients are shocked at how simple the non-qualified mortgage process is once they wrap their brains around it. And for those business owners who don't like to provide a whole bunch of documentation or income proof, this loan is the way to go. Whether you are new to investing or have been around the block, non-qualified mortgages allow you to acquire more without the headache and are the only sensible solution at this unprecedented time.

Want my help? Book a complimentary "Dream Funding Plan" at the website listed below.

On this call, I will...

*** Learn your investment or funding goals.**
*** Suggest best practice options according to your goals.**
*** Help you avoid pitfalls and common mistakes that sabotage approvals.**
*** Give you a clear path of action so you can get funding with confidence.**
*** Provide you with my best recommendations and direct you to the best resources, even if I'm not the best option.**

Book Your Complimentary "Dream Funding Plan" at: www.AmandasDreamFundingPlan.com

CHAPTER SEVEN

HARD MONEY LENDING

So what exactly is hard money lending? This type of loan is facilitated by individuals, such as investors, who take the capital they have and lend out money on a case-by-case basis. It comes at a price, but it is a quick way to get a loan done because you bypass the pre-qualification process and stringent documentation associated with traditional bank loans. While conventional loans look at your credit score, history, and debt to income ratios, hard money lenders give the money based on collateral securing the loan. For example, they look at the house's value and whether or not it is worth what they are trying to purchase it for. If so, they pay for the home and put a lien on the property to ensure they get their money back, similar to how a bank would.

Hard money lending is an excellent route for someone dedicated to getting into a home quickly or looking to start investing and flipping houses. Perhaps you make a substantial amount of money, but you don't want to alter your taxes or pay more to the IRS. Hard money lending does require more skin in the game in terms of 25% to 30% down, but you can get the home quickly and not worry about adjusting your taxes until further down the line if you go the traditional lending route later. If you are an investor, it's a great short-term "fix and flip" loan to turn around and make a profit.

Hard money lending does not come without drawbacks. As mentioned, 25% to 30% down is required, and the interest rates will be in the double digits, making this a strict, short-term loan as opposed to a 30-year type scenario. You can think of it as paying a premium for convenience and speed, avoiding the mountains of paperwork, headaches, and underwriting process of traditional loans. The investors are focused on the house as collateral versus your background and what kind of borrower you are. After all, this can be pretty lucrative for them when you think about 11% interest rates. Even if it all goes south, the lender takes the time to feel safe and secure about the property, knowing that they picked it up for a good deal.

I used to work with a guy who is a loan officer, a real estate agent, and owns his own hard money lending company. So he had the benefit of dabbling in both areas and was very knowledgeable about loans and the value of homes. I set him up with a friend of mine who was doing a flip, and he was more than happy to do that loan because the house was in a desirable area. As a hard money lender, he could set up his own terms with the borrower. For example, if the house wasn't completed in the agreed-upon six months, he could come in and take it. Since hard money lenders are using their own cash, they aren't going to be frivolous. It is treated like any other business deal with set expectations and terms.

When searching for a hard money lender, most investment companies and loan officers can steer you in the right direction and introduce you to people. Sometimes loan officers will even get a commission off the referral. Alternatively, you can Google hard money lending companies in your area and interview a few based on your specific needs. Ask questions about interest rates, terms, and the length of the loans offered. Each company will offer slightly different variations, but finding a lender should be a relatively easy task.

Once you have a short-term hard money loan established, you can bridge it into a traditional mortgage for a long-term solution. Let's say you are self-employed, but you don't have two years of history. At the same time, you are making really good money in your business. Even if you are absolutely killing it in terms of income, a traditional lender will not give you a loan based on one year of taxes. But one year of being in business and a solid down payment WILL get you a loan with a hard money company. Many people in this position use the opportunity to get into the home, make payments to the hard money company, prepare themselves via taxes, and work toward the two-year history. At that point, they can come back to a loan officer who will help them transition into traditional lending.

Especially with the current market of low inventory, faster is better when getting the home you want. Hard money lending is a great way to take advantage and not miss an opportunity. Whether you are a budding entrepreneur or an investor eager to flip, hard money lending gives you just the right amount of purchasing power to reach your goals.

Want my help? Book a complimentary "Dream Funding Plan" at the website listed below.

On this call, I will...

*** Learn your investment or funding goals.**
*** Suggest best practice options according to your goals.**
*** Help you avoid pitfalls and common mistakes that sabotage approvals.**
*** Give you a clear path of action so you can get funding with confidence.**
*** Provide you with my best recommendations and direct you to the best resources, even if I'm not the best option.**

Book Your Complimentary "Dream Funding Plan" at: www.AmandasDreamFundingPlan.com

CHAPTER EIGHT

THE LOAN PROCESS

Some people think that once you sign the documents handed to you by your loan officer, the loan process is complete. In reality, it is just the beginning. As a first-time homebuyer, it is helpful to understand the loan process from start to finish and the benefits of meeting with a mortgage professional before going out and looking at homes.

STEP ONE: Pre-Qualification

Pre-qualification is very important because a real estate agent doesn't want to take you to see homes that are outside of your qualification. It can also lead to disappointment for you, as the buyer, when you fall in love with more amenities, luxury items, or square footage, only to find out that the house is $100,000 more than what you qualify for. A loan officer will give you a target price range, avoiding false hope and letdowns along the way.

Buying a home is most likely the largest purchase you will ever make, which can be highly stressful. Finding a loan officer who responds quickly and explains things clearly will alleviate much fear and anxiety. The first thing your loan officer will do is ask you to fill out an application and provide proper income documentation to verify the exact price category you will fall into. If a loan officer tells you that you qualify for something without looking at your documentation, run the other way. Going through the income documentation process is crucial, especially since people get paid in many different ways. Truck drivers, for example, get paid by payload, making their income variable. Then we have to look at the bigger picture to obtain the correct purchase amount. You deserve to be matched with a home value that reflects your income, so choose a loan officer that will prioritize pre-qualification.

STEP TWO: Meet With a Real Estate Agent

Loan officers have many great connections to real estate agents. They can match you with someone based on personality, how they will run a contract, or how aggressive they are. If you already have a real estate agent in mind, you can take the lead and introduce the agent to your loan officer and let them get to work. Behind the scenes, they will work closely to coordinate a smooth and easy home buying process. Especially in a competitive market, they will strategize to win contracts, which is necessary to you as the buyer. Once you find a home that you would like to put an offer on, the real estate agent will ask for your pre-qualification letter.

They typically want the letter to reflect what you will offer, not what your maximum amount is, so as not to reveal all the cards in their hand at once.

STEP THREE: Under Contract

Once you're under contract, things will start to move pretty quickly. The loan officer will submit the loan, and initial disclosures will be sent out to you. When you sign these disclosures, keep in mind that they do not hold you to anything. It isn't like signing your life away. These signatures simply allow the company to start working on your file and order the items that need to be done immediately, such as the appraisal. The numbers may change if you decide to put more money down or haven't locked down the exact rate yet. But at this time, just sign the documents to get the ball rolling - there is nothing to be concerned about.

STEP FOUR: Processing

Loan processing goes a bit deeper than the initial pre-qualification process. More documentation could be required as we pull the title, there could be a lien on your name that nobody knew about, or perhaps someone owes child support, and it didn't show up on the credit report. Things come up, and we have to be prepared to deal with each circumstance. A great loan processor will also anticipate what the underwriter is going to want based on the specific file. Some items and documents are standard throughout the process, while others will be unique to you. The processor will provide you with a list of additional items needed to satisfy the particular loan program you have chosen. In the loan business, 24 hours is the equivalent of a week. Appraisals and titles need to be ordered rapidly, and additional documentation needs to be provided quickly. Many third-party people are working on your loan as well, such as homeowner's insurance companies. So the loan process will go as fast or as slowly as you (the borrower) will allow. The sooner you provide documents when asked, the sooner your loan enters the next phase.

STEP FIVE: Underwriting

The underwriter goes through your entire file with a fine-tooth comb. It is their job to verify that you have met all of the guidelines. If there are any scenarios, such as you being laid off for some time, the underwriter will dig deeper into those instances. The underwriter is held at a high level of accountability for the loan and takes excellent care in reviewing the file. Some underwriters are fantastic to work with and willing to help you meet your goals, while others can be more difficult. The end goal is to come up with a clean, simple file with no red flags. After it comes out of underwriting, your loan is considered "conditionally approved."

If something was missed, it doesn't mean your chances of moving forward in the process are ruined. The file would be sent back to processing, and the loan processor would tell you what items are needed to solve the issue.

STEP SIX: Clearing Underwriting

At this point, your loan officer will come back to you with an additional set of required documentation from the underwriter. If they have done their job well, it should only be a few more items. You may have guessed by now that speed is critical when getting these items to your loan officer. The documents will be sent back to the underwriter for a second review, and the finish line is now in sight.

STEP SEVEN: Clear to Close

The underwriter will tie up loose ends and verify that each loan condition has been met. Everyone in the industry anxiously awaits to hear those words, "CLEAR TO CLOSE."

STEP EIGHT: Document Preparation

A separate team sets up the final figures with the title company. You will receive your final closing disclosure, which you will sign with the understanding of how much money is required for your down payment and what the official interest rate is. This document is crucial because it is time-sensitive. It is a pivotal point in the process, as you cannot close on your home until three days *after* the document is signed. There isn't much room for hesitation here. The quicker you can sign, the faster you will arrive at your closing date. While this is happening, the closing and funding department is preparing your paperwork, balancing your CD, and making sure that every fee, every lender credit, and every penny is accounted for.

STEP NINE: Closing and Signing

Closing and signing occur when you meet with the title company, real estate agent, and loan officer to sit down and sign your documents. A few things will happen during this time, including the wire transfer. Once the wire transfer has arrived at the title company, it must be recorded with the county.

Many borrowers might think that since the documents are signed, now is the time to make big purchases like furniture for their new home. I must warn you - now is NOT the time. Doing so can impede or even kill the whole deal. You must wait until the "fund and record" after the title company takes the deed and records it with the county. THEN, you are officially done and can enjoy a trip to IKEA with credit cards in hand.

STEP TEN: Congratulations! You Are Officially a Homeowner!

Want my help? Book a complimentary "Dream Funding Plan" at the website listed below.

On this call, I will...

*** Learn your investment or funding goals.**
*** Suggest best practice options according to your goals.**
*** Help you avoid pitfalls and common mistakes that sabotage approvals.**
*** Give you a clear path of action so you can get funding with confidence.**
*** Provide you with my best recommendations and direct you to the best resources, even if I'm not the best option.**

Book Your Complimentary "Dream Funding Plan" at:
www.AmandasDreamFundingPlan.com

THE TIME IS NOW...

As a self-employed borrower, you have learned what it takes to qualify financially and the importance of working with a skilled CPA and loan officer team. Depending on your particular business, you can determine if a CPA, accountant, or bookkeeper is right for you. Additionally, you are aware of the loan options available to you, whether traditional, non-qualified, or hard money lending.

My passion is helping the self-employed navigate the path to homeownership. It is about so much more than the house itself. Homeownership leads to a vast portfolio of equity, financial stability, and opportunities to become an investor. As a business owner, you can then build your wealth at a higher capacity. Now is the time to buy. Don't hesitate. Set yourself up for success and use the insight from these pages to purchase the home of your dreams or become an investor, creating passive income that will dramatically change your life and the way you do business.

ABOUT AMANDA MADSEN "THE MAVERICK MORTGAGE MAVEN"

Amanda Madsen started working in customer satisfaction in 1994. In 1997 she began consulting others, and in 2000, she took her entrepreneurial spirit and started her first company. As a self-employed single mom, Amanda's determination and drive pushed her through to become one of the top salon owners in the state of Utah. Her passion for helping others achieve their dreams led her to the real estate world, and in 2011, she took on a new adventure and became a loan officer.

Amanda's understanding of self-employment, life experience, and tenacity to see a project through helped her earn the title of "Mortgage Wizard" from her most trusted clients. Amanda's background in self-employment has been the driving force to help others that are self-employed get into homeownership and investments. Amanda seems to be able to pull off the impossible. Her

work ethic and integrity have allowed her to become one of the best lenders to work with in the United States. She loves the outdoors, camping, traveling, yoga, horseback riding, and of course, her mastiffs Sable and Ares.

She is truly the expert when it comes to getting a loan done, especially for the self-employed.

WHAT AMANDA'S CLIENTS ARE SAYING

As a self-employed real estate agent, working with Amanda is so fun and helps me look good to my clients. She brings more of a team approach which keeps the client and the agent all in the loop. She takes the time to work with my self-employed clients to guide them through the process and explain how to approach the income for their home purchasing needs. We game plan and come up with solid ideas in these times of multiple offer situations to get the win for our clients. It is so important to work with a lender that knows what they are talking about and is willing to do what is needed even on a late weekend night. Working with Amanda you can trust that you have a professional looking out for your best interest. I would never recommend anyone I have never used myself because it could hurt my reputation. I have used Amanda to purchase and refinance, trust me when I say they were smooth easy transactions.

-Chase Stam, Realtor

Amanda is an incredible person and an outstanding Mortgage Loan Originator.

Her drive and determination for success is clear. Her attention to detail is impeccable. Her loyalty and trust are undeniably solid and her sense of ease to calm any situation is reassuring. She is solution-oriented and very creative. Amanda will go above and beyond to make sure you are well taken care of and she can get you the best rates possible.

I have always had my own business and have found it challenging to work with your conventional Mortgage broker. I've been told by a handful that they are unable to either get me qualified or come back with huge interest rates, etc. Amanda takes her work to a whole other level and is highly educated and continues to push herself to make whatever arrangements possible to get the deal done for you.

I highly recommend Amanda.

- Sara Clemensen, Garden Girls Utah

As a self-employed person, my situation in refinancing five properties and a new purchase was a bit complicated yet Amanda was able to make it happen in a timely manner. She was very supportive and available to help me get through the process. The e-sign process is great and so much more simple. My escrow company was impressed.

- Wayne Sharp, Entrepreneur and Real Estate Investor

"Amanda the Wizard"

This is my story about how I've been able to excel financially in my life because of who I now call my financial wizard. When I returned home from my LDS mission I was encouraged by my dad to buy an investment property and to live in it so it could pay itself off and I would have my mortgage paid for by someone else and I was excited there was someone in my neighborhood that worked for a lending office who said I would be able to get a loan for a house. I returned home from my mission in 2011 and right away tried to buy a duplex for $210,000. I went under contract for it. My earnest money went hard and I was assured by the lender that I was able to get this property and we eventually extended the closing date three weeks beyond what I was originally told because financing wasn't going to happen because I didn't have two years of previous work history. So I lost that property and then two weeks later I went under contract for another property that was for less money and I was still assured by the company that I was able to get the loan. My earnest money went hard again and we extended it two more weeks and still wasn't able to get that loan and that mortgage brokerage said that they would pay an extra $500 in earnest money because they were sure that I was able to get the loan and they lost their $500 in the end as well. So I gave up on buying properties until I had two years of work history.

And then came Amanda. I found her through a networking group and she was the most persistent saleswoman I've ever dealt with. She kept calling me and calling me and promised me that I was able to get a loan and I told her that there was no way because I just tried and lost $1200-$2000 in earnest money and inspections because I paid inspections on both of the properties as well. But she was very sure that she could get me a loan and so I eventually trusted her and she got me properties in the next eight months without two years of work history. That's when she got her title as mortgage wizard in my books and I tell everyone that I have a wizard that can come up with money out of nowhere. I don't know how she does it; she just is always able to overcome any problems that arise. Because of this I now have refinanced purchased homes and have gotten somewhere between 12 to 15 loans or refinances with her. I'm self-employed and I know there's nowhere else that would be able to do this.

The first property that I bought has given me a huge jump in my financial life and I am way further than anybody my age because of Amanda. She's always willing to explain everything to me. She's the most patient person because being self-employed I always have other things that I feel that are more important and she's very knowledgeable on how to get money out of thin air. We're to the point where I tell her I want this to happen and she figures it out somehow. Anybody that I know that is even thinking about buying a property I tell them that they need to use the wizard or they'll regret their decisions of using another loan officer. Now I have multiple properties that subsidize my other businesses as they are growing and going through tough times. Because of Amanda I have a confident goal of having enough passive income by 40 through real estate to be able to retire if I wanted to. But why stop there?

- Tyler Sharp, Entrepreneur and Real Estate Investor

Made in the USA
Monee, IL
04 November 2026

67376099R00059